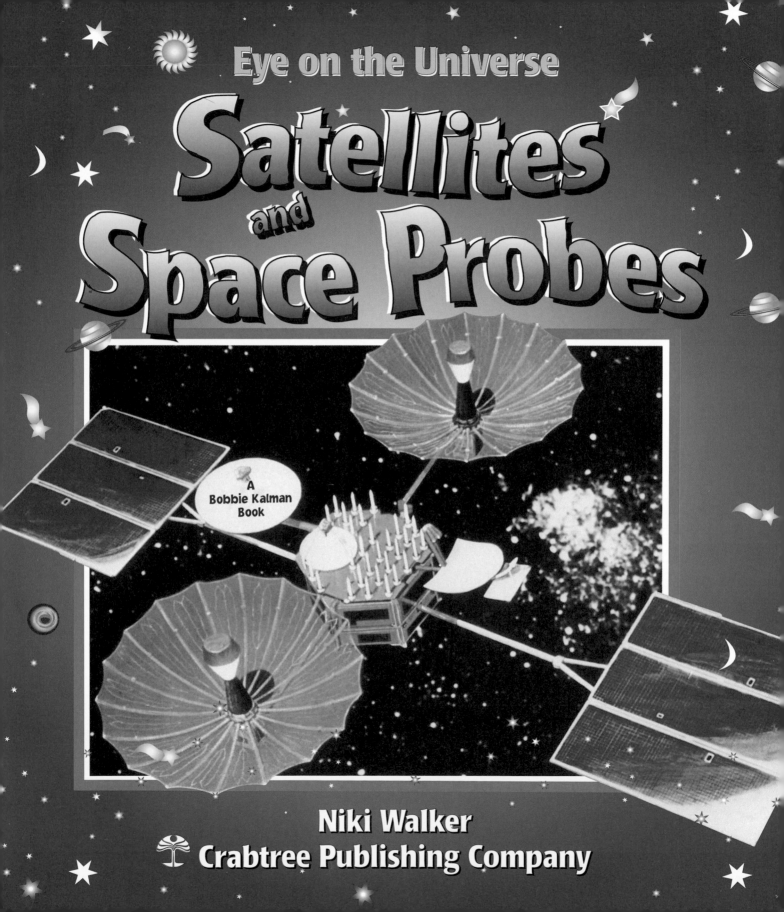

Eye on the Universe

Satellites and Space Probes

A Bobbie Kalman Book

Niki Walker
Crabtree Publishing Company

Eye on the Universe

Created by Bobbie Kalman

For Hannelore—there are no limits

Editor-in-Chief
Bobbie Kalman

Written by
Niki Walker

Managing editor
Lynda Hale

Editors
Jacqueline Langille
April Fast
Hannelore Sotzek

Computer design
Lynda Hale
Lucy DeFazio
Campbell Creative Services

Production coordinator
Hannelore Sotzek

Consultant
Jurrie J. van der Woude,
Jet Propulsion Lab, NASA

Special thanks to
Jurrie J. van der Woude, Jet Propulsion Lab, NASA; Adrienne Wasserman, United States Geological Survey; Jim Sahli, Goddard Space Flight Center; Debra L. Dodds, NASA; Elizabeth "Betsy" Carter, Ames Research Center, NASA; Ian Gordon, Science Library, Brock University; Nicola Hill

Photographs
Warren Faidley/Weatherstock: page 13 (bottom)
Bobbie Kalman: page 11
NASA: pages 8, 10, 13 (top), 17 (top), 26
NASA/Ames Research Center: page 23
NASA/JPL: pages 5 (bottom), 6, 20, 21, 22, 31 (both)
NASA/STScI/AURA: page 17 (bottom both)
Photo Researchers, Inc.:
   Julian Baum/Science Photo Library: page 27 (top)
   David Ducros/Science Photo Library: page 5 (top left)
   David A. Hardy/Science Photo Library: page 5 (top right)
   NASA/Science Photo Library: page 27 (bottom)
   Novosti Press Agency/Science Photo Library: page 23 (bottom)
Photri, Inc.: page 29 (both)
Other photographs by Digital Stock and Digital Vision

Illustrations
All illustrations by Barbara Bedell

Crabtree Publishing Company

350 Fifth Avenue	360 York Road, RR 4,	73 Lime Walk
Suite 3308	Niagara-on-the-Lake,	Headington
New York	Ontario, Canada	Oxford OX3 7AD
N.Y. 10118	L0S 1J0	United Kingdom

Cataloging in Publication Data
Walker, Niki
   Satellites and space probes

(Eye on the universe)
Includes index.

ISBN 0-86505-681-1 (library bound)   ISBN 0-86505-691-9 (pbk.)
This book introduces basic types of artificial satellites, the mechanics of launching into space, and the history and accomplishments of specific spacecraft including the Hubble Space Telescope, Galileo, and Cassini.

1. Artificial satellites—Juvenile literature. 2. Space probes—Juvenile literature. [1. Artificial satellites. 2. Space probes.] I. Title. II. Series: Kalman, Bobbie. Eye on the universe.

TL793.3.W35 1998   j629.43   LC 98-3308
                                                          CIP

Contents

Satellites and space probes

Spacecraft are vehicles that travel into space. They can be rockets or space shuttles. Some are **satellites**. Others are scientific vehicles that carry **space probes**. Spacecraft often are sent towards a target such as the Moon. Many are sent to orbit the Earth and other planets.

Atmosphere and space

Where the **atmosphere** ends, space begins. The atmosphere is a layer of gases that surrounds Earth. It protects Earth from heat and cold. Part of the atmosphere, the **ozone layer**, stops many of the sun's dangerous rays from reaching Earth. The gases in the atmosphere make up air. Near the ground, in the **troposphere**, the air is very dense and easy to breathe. Space begins where there is hardly any air, about 100 miles (160 km) above the ground. Without space suits, astronauts could not breathe.

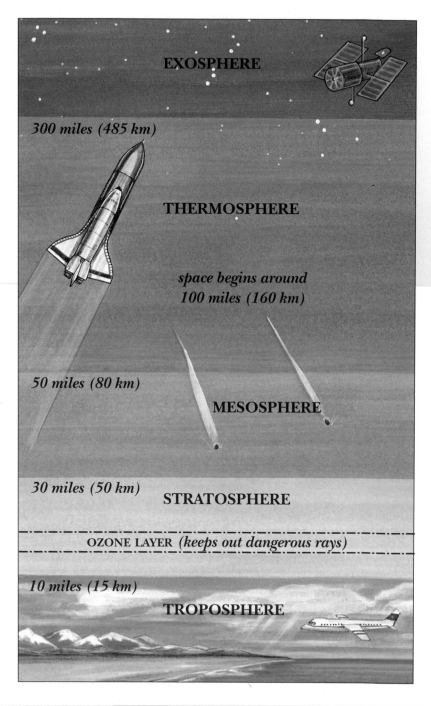

EXOSPHERE

300 miles (485 km)

THERMOSPHERE

space begins around 100 miles (160 km)

50 miles (80 km)

MESOSPHERE

30 miles (50 km)

STRATOSPHERE

OZONE LAYER *(keeps out dangerous rays)*

10 miles (15 km)

TROPOSPHERE

What is a satellite?

A satellite is an object that **orbits**, or travels around, a planet. The Moon is a natural satellite of Earth. **Artificial satellites** are machines that are sent into space by people. They orbit Earth and carry out a variety of jobs. Hundreds of artificial satellites are orbiting Earth right now!

The first spacecraft

In 1957, the former Soviet Union launched the first artificial satellite. It was called *Sputnik 1*, shown above. It was 23 inches (58 cm) across and weighed 405 pounds (184 kg). Even though *Sputnik 1* did little more than make a beeping sound, its launch began the **Space Age**. The Space Age is the name given to the last few decades of our century, during which, people have been exploring space with spacecraft.

What are space probes?

Space probes are robots that are carried to other parts of our solar system by scientific spacecraft. They send back information about the planets, Sun, Moon, and even about space itself. They also send back pictures. Almost everything we know about our solar system was discovered by space probes.

Launching a spacecraft

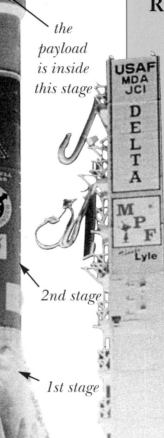

the *payload is inside this stage*

2nd stage

1st stage

USAF MDA JCI DELTA M P F I Lyle

Both satellites and scientific spacecraft need a powerful "boost" to get past the edge of the atmosphere and become true spacecraft. They are **launched**, or lifted into space, by rockets or space shuttles. A satellite or probe is called a **payload** when it is being carried aboard one of these launch vehicles.

Escape from Earth

In order to escape the pull of Earth's gravity, a vehicle must travel incredibly fast—at least 24,000 miles (40 000 km) an hour! This speed is called **escape velocity**.

Riding a rocket

Most rockets, such as the one on the left, are **multistage rockets**. They are made up of two or more rockets. The first **stage**, or rocket, fires on the ground. It pushes the rocket almost to the edge of the atmosphere before it runs out of fuel and drops away. The second stage then fires and shoots the rocket into space. The third stage carries the payload even higher and then falls away. The payload is then sent into orbit.

A rocket engine is filled almost completely with fuel. As this fuel burns, it causes a burst of hot gases to shoot from the bottom of the rocket. As the gases shoot out, they force the rocket upward.

The space shuttle

Rockets are huge, expensive spacecraft that can be used only once. The space shuttle can be used again and again. It is a cross between a rocket and an airplane. It has a huge fuel tank and two booster rockets that lift it into space. The boosters help launch the shuttle and then fall away. The external fuel tank fuels the shuttle for 9 minutes, and then it also falls away. The **orbiter**, which resembles an airplane, is the main vehicle. It carries astronauts and the payload into space. The payload is carried in the cargo bay. Once the shuttle reaches space, the cargo bay doors open and the payload is **deployed**, or lifted overboard, by a huge robotic arm. The orbiter then moves away.

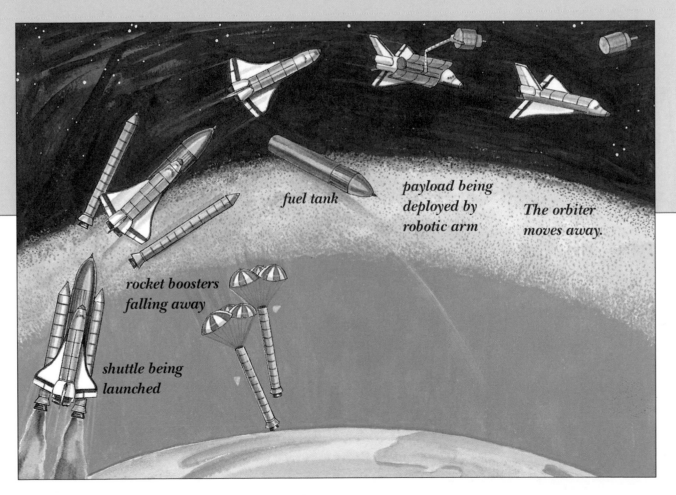

fuel tank

payload being deployed by robotic arm

The orbiter moves away.

rocket boosters falling away

shuttle being launched

Why don't satellites fall?

More than 300 years ago—long before spacecraft were invented—a scientist named Sir Isaac Newton figured out how an object could orbit the Earth. The pictures on the right illustrate his ideas. Newton figured that if an object high above the Earth was moving fast enough, it would never land. Even though gravity pulled on it, a satellite would travel too quickly to be pulled down to Earth's surface. Instead, it would travel in a curved path all the way around the planet.

Staying up

People had no way of testing Newton's ideas at the time but, hundreds of years later, scientists proved that Newton was right about orbits! To orbit the Earth, a satellite must travel at least 17,000 miles (27 000 km) an hour. A spacecraft must be at least 95 miles (150 km) above the Earth's surface to stay in orbit. At this height, the atmosphere is so thin that air does not tug on the satellite and slow it below orbit speed. Once a satellite is in orbit, it does not need much power to stay there.

Fired up

Satellites and space probes have small remote-controlled rockets called **boosters**. After a satellite or probe is deployed, the crew at a ground station commands it to fire its boosters. The boosters push the spacecraft farther into space and increase its speed so that it is not pulled back to Earth by gravity.

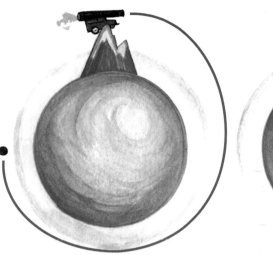

According to Newton, a cannon-ball shot with some force from an imaginary mountaintop above the atmosphere would fall back to Earth.

If the cannonball were shot with greater force, it would travel so fast that it would never land. It would travel all the way around Earth in orbit.

The Space Shuttle shows how Newton's idea works. By traveling at high speed above Earth's atmosphere, the shuttle can send a satellite into orbit.

What a drag!

When a satellite does not move fast enough, Earth's gravity pulls it toward the atmosphere. The satellite skims along the edge of the atmosphere, and air pushes against it, slowing it even more. Air slowing the satellite is called **drag**. As drag slows the satellite, gravity pulls it even farther into the atmosphere. As it falls, the air rubbing against it makes it so hot that it burns. Most satellites burn up completely before reaching the ground.

Drag and gravity can pull a satellite that is not moving fast enough out of orbit.

9

Satellite jobs

ost satellites are designed and built to perform one main task. There are six basic types of satellites circling the Earth—communication, resource, navigation, military, scientific, and weather satellites.

Navigation satellites

Navigation satellites are used by sailors and pilots to help them **navigate**, or find their way. They also help boats and planes in emergencies. They receive distress signals and send them to rescue stations.

Sending messages

To stay in touch with spacecraft, scientists use **radio waves** like the ones that carry music to your radio. Radio waves travel through air and can carry information about sounds and pictures. The information must be turned into a special code before it can be sent or received, however. A radio wave carrying this coded information is called a **radio signal**.

Navigation satellites send out signals that are picked up by equipment on airplanes and boats. A computer then uses the signals to tell the pilot or captain exactly where the plane or boat is.

Keeping in touch

Communication satellites help people all over the world stay in touch with one another. They relay radio broadcasts, telephone calls, and television programs from one side of the world to the other in a matter of seconds.

(right) This girl can watch television on a boat in the middle of the ocean because of a communication satellite such as the one below.

A **ground station** is a place on Earth that stays in contact with satellites. Transmitters and antennas relay signals between the stations and satellites

After a communication satellite receives a signal, it makes the signal stronger and sends it down to a ground station on another part of Earth.

antenna

transmitter

signals sent to satellite

signals sent from satellite

ground station in North America

ground station in Europe

Watchful "eyes"

From high above Earth, satellites have a good view of what is happening below them. Their view is useful for gathering intelligence and studying weather and resources such as forests.

Military satellites

The armed forces have their own system of satellites. They use it for navigation, communication, and **reconnaissance**. Reconnaissance satellites are used to gather information on other governments.

Resource satellites

Resource satellites help scientists monitor natural resources and the environment. They take pictures of the Earth's surface. The pictures are used to make maps and search for underground resources such as oil. They also help scientists keep track of ocean life, study the growth of crops, and watch the spread of droughts and forest fires. The pictures taken by resource satellites often show air and water pollution as well.

Weather satellites

Weather satellites, called **meteorological satellites**, carry cameras that photograph the Earth's atmosphere and clouds. Scientists study the pictures taken by these satellites to see what kinds of clouds are in the atmosphere. They can tell where snow or rain is falling, storms are forming, and in which direction the clouds causing this weather are going. The picture on the left shows a hurricane cloud. Can you see its "eye?"

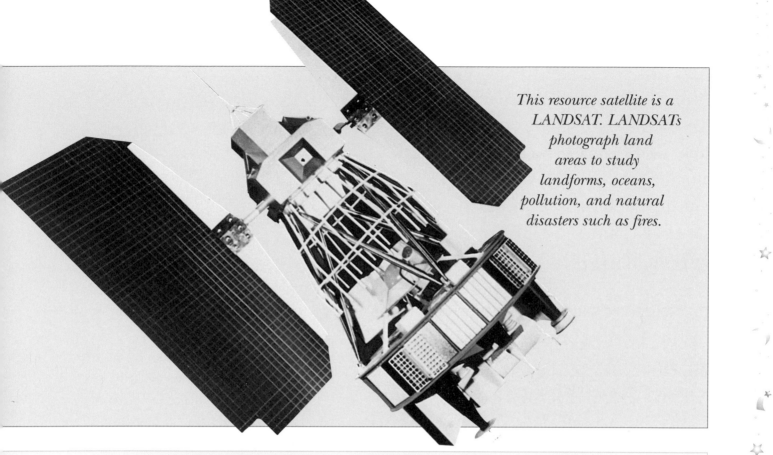

This resource satellite is a LANDSAT. LANDSATs photograph land areas to study landforms, oceans, pollution, and natural disasters such as fires.

Time to prepare

In the past, people were often caught off guard by hurricanes, tornadoes, blizzards, and other dangerous weather. Thanks to weather satellites, forecasters can now warn people when a storm is approaching so they can prepare for it.

Boarding up windows and doors helps protect a house from high winds.

Scientific satellites

It is difficult to study space from Earth. The atmosphere affects the quality of the images people can see through a telescope. Scientists use scientific satellites to see images more clearly and to learn more about conditions in space.

Many scientific satellites study the conditions of space near Earth and the relationship between the Sun, Earth, and the rest of space. Other satellites study deep space.

Space stations

A **space station** is a large satellite that is designed to have people living and working aboard it for weeks or months at a time. Astronauts on a space station perform many scientific experiments. They themselves are experiments! Scientists watch how their bodies are affected by being in space for several months. So far, three space stations have been launched—*Salyut*, Skylab, and *Mir*. *Mir* is the only one still in use. It has been in space more than 10 years.

Skylab

Skylab orbited Earth from 1971 to 1979, but astronauts worked on board only in 1973. There were three crews, each made up of three astronauts who lived on the station and performed experiments in the lab. In 1979, Skylab fell out of orbit and burned in the Earth's atmosphere. Parts of it crashed in the Indian Ocean and in Australia.

Skylab, shown left, was launched by the United States. It was the largest artificial satellite ever to orbit Earth.

Space station *Mir*

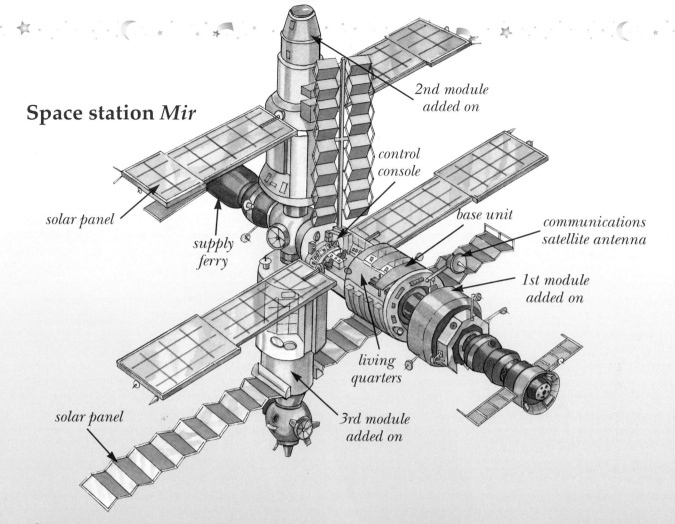

2nd module added on

control console

solar panel

supply ferry

base unit

communications satellite antenna

1st module added on

living quarters

solar panel

3rd module added on

The Russian space station *Mir* was launched in 1986. On *Mir*, Russian astronauts, called *cosmonauts*, live and work alongside astronauts from other countries. A space shuttle carries astronauts and supplies to and from *Mir*.

Since it has been in orbit, *Mir* has experienced a number of serious problems, such as a broken door latch and trouble with its oxygen generators. In 1992, a supply ship smashed into *Mir* and poked a hole into one of its modules, causing *Mir* to spin out of control. The astronauts had only ten seconds to seal off the damaged module before all the air rushed out. Later that year, a computer problem caused *Mir*'s solar panels to move away from the sun. *Mir* had to be steered back to its original position. It was without power until its solar batteries were recharged.

Although *Mir* has had many problems, it has taught the world a lot about the universe and helped people learn how to live in space for long periods of time. The new International Space Station, which will replace *Mir*, is scheduled to be completed in 1999.

The Hubble Space Telescope

Clouds, dust, pollution, and the lights of towns and cities limit the view of space that scientists have from the ground. The Hubble Space Telescope is a satellite that was launched to give scientists a bigger, clearer view of our solar system and the universe beyond it. The telescope was launched aboard the space shuttle Discovery on April 25, 1990. Scientists expect the Hubble to work for at least fifteen years.

The Hubble could pick up the beam of a flashlight 250,000 miles (400 000 km) away—the distance from Earth to the Moon!

*Hubble is "on" 24 hours a day, but it does not spend all its time looking through the universe and taking pictures. The telescope spends some time each day **housekeeping**. Housekeeping tasks include turning to avoid the bright light of the Sun or Moon, sending information down to Earth, and receiving commands.*

Repairs in space

As soon as the Hubble began sending back pictures, scientists knew that there was a problem with one of the mirrors. The mirrors are needed to create clear pictures. Luckily, the Hubble was designed to be repaired in space. In 1993, a crew of astronauts made repairs to correct the faulty mirror. To make sure that the Hubble keeps working properly, **servicing missions** are scheduled to take place every three years. During these missions, worn or damaged parts will be repaired or replaced.

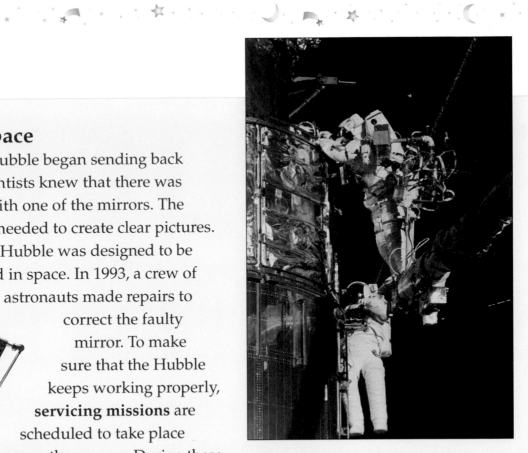

The Hubble Space Telescope can be repaired easily because it has ladders that astronauts can climb as they work.

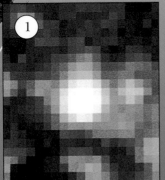

1. Image of stars seen through a telescope on Earth

2. Image of stars taken by the Hubble Space Telescope

View of the universe

The Hubble travels 370 miles (595 km) above Earth's surface. From this height, it has a clear view of almost the entire universe. It can see a thousand times farther and ten times more clearly than the most powerful telescope on Earth. It is able to create sharp pictures of objects that are several billion **light-years** away! A light year is the distance light travels in one year—6 trillion miles (10 trillion km).

Satellite paths

The satellites orbiting Earth travel in one of several **orbits**, or paths around the planet. A satellite's orbit depends on the job the satellite has to do. The illustrations here show the different paths satellites can take. Most satellites are found in a band that is between 300 and 23,000 miles (485 km and 37 000 km) above Earth's surface.

Satellite spotting

Some satellites travel so close to Earth that they can be seen without using a telescope. The best time to spot a satellite is just after sunset or just before sunrise. Watch the sky near the horizon for a "star" moving in a slow, steady line across the sky. The star is actually a satellite! The satellite's metal body and big solar panels reflect sunlight, making it appear as bright as a star.

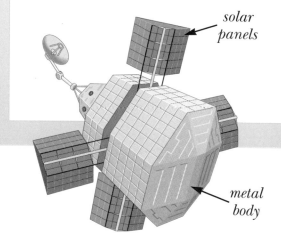

solar panels

metal body

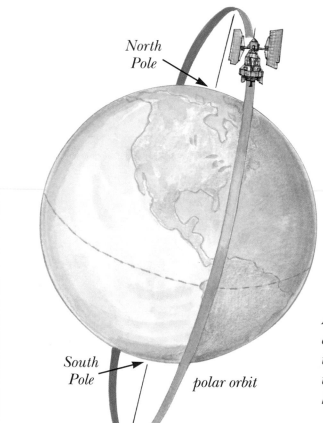

North Pole

South Pole

polar orbit

*A satellite in a **polar orbit** travels from pole to pole around the Earth. The Earth turns on its axis while the satellite moves from the north pole to the south and then returns to the north pole. In a period of 24 hours, the satellite sees every spot on Earth.*

elliptical orbit

An **elliptical orbit** takes a satellite far from Earth at one end and very close to Earth at the other. This orbit is useful for scientific satellites.

A satellite in a **geosynchronous orbit** moves at the same speed as the Earth's rotation. Since the satellite and Earth move at the same rate, the satellite is always above the same spot on Earth's surface. It appears to be "parked" even though it is moving. Most communication satellites and many weather satellites use this orbit.

geosynchronous orbit

Long-distance information

In the late 1950s, **NASA**, the United States's space agency, and the former Soviet Union's space agency began launching scientific spacecraft carrying space probes. In the past 40 years, probes have traveled throughout much of our solar system. They have gathered information and sent back thousands of images of planets and their moons. Pluto is the only planet in the solar system that a probe has not yet explored.

Space probe point of view

Probes offer us a close-up view of planets and moons that are millions or even billions of miles away. Thanks to probes, we have seen

- Mercury's craggy, cratered surface
- Venus's thick, cloudy atmosphere
- Mars's craters, canyons, and volcanoes
- Jupiter's swirling atmosphere
- volcanoes erupting on Io, one of Jupiter's moons
- Saturn's rings up close
- the Moon's surface, shown left

The object and the camera are both moving through space. In order to get a close-up, the camera takes a series of pictures as it moves. The pictures are pieced together by a computer operator on Earth.

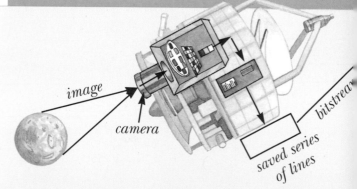

image

camera

saved series of lines

bitstream

Space probes have a camera, computer, and radio. The image taken by the camera is saved onto a computer chip as a series of lines. The computer changes the lines into a digital code.

The Deep Space Network

The radio signals sent to Earth by a space probe are received by one of three huge dish-shaped antennas. These antennas are connected to ground stations. Together, they make up the Deep Space Network, or DSN. The DSN's stations are located in California, Spain, and Australia. They are evenly spaced around the world so that one of the antennas is always able to pick up a probe's signal. The Deep Space Network not only receives radio signals, however. It also sends commands to probes and **tracks**, or follows, them.

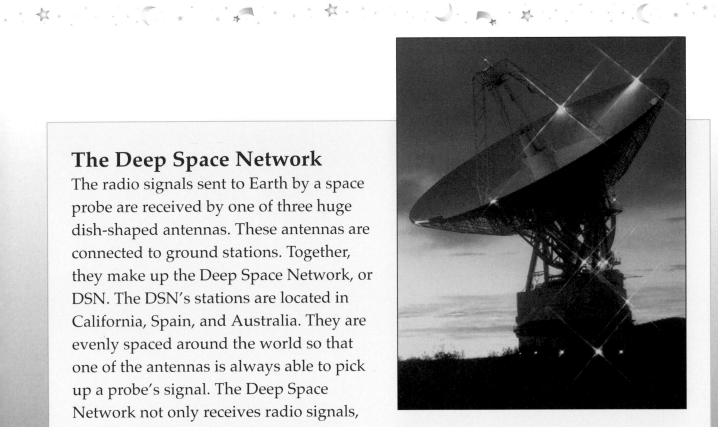

This antenna, located in California, is like a big "ear" listening for information from space.

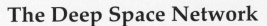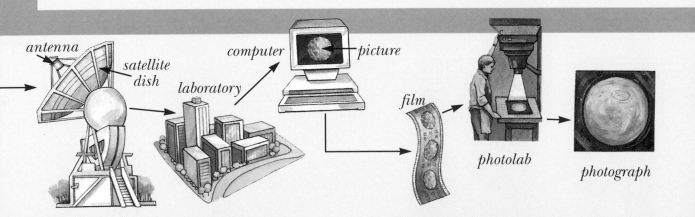

The radio sends this code through space as a bitstream to a satellite dish on earth. Antennas on a satellite dish receive the stream of information. The data is then sent to a laboratory.

*Computers in the laboratory **reformat**, or change, the information into a picture. This picture is recorded onto film, which is sent to a photolab and made into a photograph.*

To the Moon

The Moon, Earth's closest neighbor, was the first target of space probes. Some probes sent to the Moon were **orbiters**. Orbiters are sent to other planets or moons and orbit them just as artificial satellites orbit Earth. Orbiters of the Moon took pictures of its surface from high above.

Other lunar spacecraft were **landers**. Landers fly to a planet or moon and land on its surface. They take pictures of its landscape and study the soil and atmosphere, if an atmosphere exists.

The U.S. Department of Defense launched Clementine in 1994. The probe found what scientists thought might be ice at the Moon's south pole.

Preparing for astronauts

NASA launched a series of probes between 1964 and 1968. They were part of Projects Ranger, Surveyor, and Lunar Orbiter. The probes took close-up images of the Moon's surface that were used to make maps of parts of the Moon. They were also used to choose landing sites for astronauts.

Ranger probes landed on the Moon. They helped prove that spacecraft could land on the Moon without disappearing into its dusty surface. They also collected information about the soil.

Lunar Prospector

There are still many things scientists do not know about the Moon, even though dozens of probes were sent there and astronauts visited it. To help answer some questions about the Moon, NASA launched an orbiter called Lunar Prospector in 1998.

Lunar Prospector's equipment has shown that there is ice at the poles of the Moon. This news and other information sent back will help scientists figure out how the Moon formed.

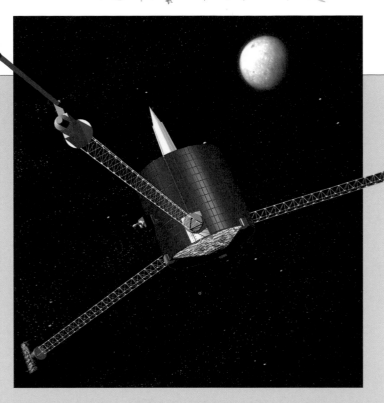

Lunar Prospector discovered that the ice on the Moon is located deep in craters, hidden from the Sun's rays.

*Lunakhod was a **surface rover**. A surface rover is a robotic vehicle that is carried to a planet or moon by a lander. Rovers give scientists a larger view of the landscape than a lander because they can move around. They can also test soil and rocks at several locations.*

Soviet probes

The former Soviet Union's lunar probes set many records. In January, 1959, Luna 1 was the first probe to leave Earth and fly past the Moon. Later that year, Luna 2 crash-landed on the Moon's surface, and Luna 3 sent back the first pictures of the Moon's **far side**. We never see the far side from Earth. In 1970, Luna 17 landed on the Moon carrying *Lunakhod*, the first remote-controlled vehicle sent to explore another world. Scientists controlled *Lunakhod* from Earth. They drove it around the Moon for eleven days, using it to collect soil samples and to take pictures.

Mercury and Venus

After scientists sent probes to the Moon, their next targets were Venus, Mars, and Mercury. Along with Earth, these planets are known as the **inner planets**. Mercury and Venus may be neighbors, but they are very different from one another. Mercury is like the Moon. It has a cratered surface and no atmosphere. Venus has a cloudy atmosphere that traps heat and makes it the hottest planet. The clouds also make it difficult for probes to take pictures of Venus's surface.

To the inner planets

In the 1960s and early 1970s, NASA launched ten scientific spacecraft to explore Venus, Mercury, and Mars. They were part of the Mariner program. One was an orbiter. The others were **flyby spacecraft**. They flew past a planet and took pictures without orbiting or landing. Mariner 10 was the first spacecraft to visit more than one planet. In 1974, it flew past Venus on its way to Mercury. It gave us our first close-up view of Mercury's surface.

The nine planets in the solar system are constantly in motion. Launching a probe so that it reaches another planet is like shooting an arrow at a moving bull's eye.

Magellan

In 1989, Magellan became the first scientific spacecraft launched by a space shuttle. It arrived at Venus in 1990. Magellan was an orbiter that circled Venus until 1994. Using radar, it completely mapped Venus's surface.

At the end of its mission, Magellan became the first probe to try **aerobraking**, or slowing down using the thin upper level of the atmosphere. When Magellan flew lower around Venus, its atmosphere dragged against the probe and slowed it so much that it was pulled in by Venus's gravity.

Many other probes have been lost or have crashed by mistake. Magellan was the first probe destroyed on purpose. Scientists wrecked Magellan in order to test aerobraking. Before the probe burned up it also sent back valuable information about Venus's atmosphere.

Mars

People once believed that the planet Venus was very similar to Earth. When spacecraft explored Venus and Mars, however, scientists came to another conclusion. Probes took images of both planets, measured their temperature, studied their atmospheres, and discovered that Mars is the planet most like Earth. Because of this discovery, Mars is the next planet that astronauts will explore.

The Viking mission

In 1975, NASA launched two scientific spacecraft to explore Mars. They were called Viking 1 and Viking 2 and were exactly the same. Each one was an orbiter spacecraft that carried a lander. It took them nearly a year to reach Mars. When they did, the landers separated from the orbiters and landed on the planet's surface.

Scientists thought the probes might stop working 90 days after they reached Mars, but they all continued to work for many years! The orbiters mapped almost the entire planet. They were able to take more than 52,000 pictures, and the landers took 4,500 images! The landers gave people the very first view of Mars's landscape.

The Viking probes were the first missions to land a spacecraft safely on the surface of another planet.

Studying Mars

Scientists are continuing their mission to study Mars. They hope that the information collected will lead to human exploration of Mars early in the next century. The mission is made up of a series of programs. The first program was the launching of an orbiter called Mars Global Surveyor in 1996. Scientists believe that it will be at least 1999 before the spacecraft is in proper orbit to collect information about the weather, atmosphere, and surface of the planet. The next program was called Mars Pathfinder. It carried a surface rover called Sojourner.

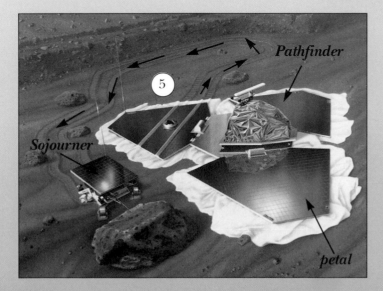

The picture above shows the stages of Pathfinder's landing on Mars.
1. The lander entered Mars's atmosphere and became very hot. 2. It released a parachute to slow itself down before it hit the ground. 3. One second before it hit the ground, the lander inflated air bags to cushion itself when it landed. 4. After reaching the surface, the lander's three protective panels, called **petals**, *opened. 5. The picture on the left shows the tiny rover, Sojourner. It used a petal as a ramp to drive down to the ground. The arrows show its tracks behind the petal.*

To the edge and beyond

In the early 1970s, NASA began sending space probes to explore the **outer planets** of the solar system. The outer planets are Jupiter, Saturn, Uranus, Neptune, and Pluto, but Pluto has not yet been studied by a space probe. The first four spacecraft sent to study the outer planets were Pioneers 10 and 11 and Voyagers 1 and 2. These spacecraft discovered information about the distant outer planets that scientists would never have been able to collect from Earth.

Pioneering probes

Pioneer 10 and 11 were the first two scientific spacecraft sent to explore the outer solar system. Pioneer 10 was launched in March, 1972, and Pioneer 11 was launched in April, 1973. Both were flyby spacecraft designed to fly past and take pictures of the outer planets. They also studied what space is like in the outer part of the solar system.

Long-distance travelers

By the end of its mission, Pioneer 10 was 6 billion miles (10 billion km) from Earth! It was the first spacecraft:
• to cross the **Asteroid Belt**—the space between Mars and Jupiter that is filled with rocks called asteroids
• to take close-up pictures of Jupiter

Pioneer 11 flew over 4 billion miles (6.5 billion km) before its mission ended. It was the first spacecraft:
• to take close-up images of Saturn and its rings
• to find two moons that scientists had not noticed from Earth

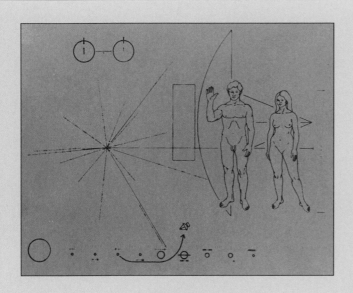

Hello out there

Pioneer 10 and 11 are the first spacecraft intended to travel into the space beyond our solar system. Scientists put a plaque with a greeting on each one, in case an alien finds the spacecraft. Voyagers 1 and 2 also carry a greeting for extraterrestrials. It is a record album with sounds from several places on Earth, as well as greetings in over 200 languages. The messages are recorded in computer language.

Voyage to the edge

Voyagers 1 and 2 were identical spacecraft launched in 1977. Their mission was to fly past Jupiter and Saturn to study the planets, their largest moons, and Saturn's rings.

A longer tour

Scientists planned for the Voyagers' tours of the solar system to last five years. The probes were so successful that scientists extended their trip. When their mission finally ended after twelve years, the Voyager spacecraft had studied all four outer planets, their rings, and more than 50 of their moons. Both probes are intended to leave the solar system and are still sending back information!

Return to the giants

The Voyager and Pioneer spacecraft to the outer planets were flyby spacecraft. Although they returned the first close-up pictures of the planets, the probes could only take images of the areas that were facing them as they flew past. They could not gather information about the surfaces, but they learned about the atmospheres and temperatures of Jupiter, Saturn, Uranus, and Neptune. NASA launched Galileo to return to Jupiter and Cassini to return to Saturn to find out more about these giant planets.

Galileo

Galileo was aimed at Jupiter, the biggest planet. It was launched in 1989 and reached its target in 1995. Galileo was an orbiter that carried an **atmospheric probe**. An atmospheric probe is carried to its target by another spacecraft, usually an orbiter. It is released above its target planet and falls through the atmosphere of that planet while the orbiter moves away to continue its own mission.

The Galileo Atmospheric Probe completed its mission when it was destroyed by the pressure and temperatures of Jupiter's atmosphere about an hour after entering it. The information it collected is still being studied by scientists.

Galileo is still orbiting Jupiter and studying the planet and its moons. Scientists will use the information it gathers to understand the discoveries made by the atmospheric probe.

Cassini

Cassini is an orbiter that was sent into space in October 1997. It is one of the largest scientific spacecraft ever launched. Cassini is expected to reach its target, Saturn, in 2004 and will study it until 2008. It has an atmospheric probe called Huygens on board.

(right) Huygens is dropped into the atmosphere of Titan, Saturn's largest moon, while Cassini moves away to orbit and study Saturn.

(below) The diagram below shows the separate sections of Huygens.

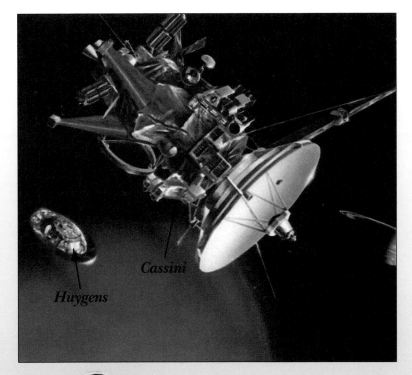

Cassini

Huygens

experiment equipment

after cone

ejection device pushes Huygens away from Cassini

front shield protects the probe as it falls through the atmosphere

back cover

top platform

fore dome

Huygens's jobs include

- measuring the **composition**, or makeup, of the gases in Titan's atmosphere
- studying Titan's clouds
- studying Titan's surface
- recording the effect of Titan's winds on itself as it falls through the atmosphere

Glossary

aerobraking The process of slowing down a spacecraft using the drag, or pull, of the atmosphere

astronaut A person who has been trained to fly aboard spacecraft

atmosphere The gases that surround a planet

Deep Space Network The network of antennas that pick up signals from space

drag Air pushing against a satellite and slowing it down

flyby spacecraft A spacecraft that cannot land on a planet's surface

geosynchronous Describing the orbit of a satellite that is moving at the same speed as Earth's rotation

gravity The force that pulls objects toward the center of a planet or moon

inner planets The planets that are closest to the Sun—Earth, Mars, Mercury, and Venus

lander A spacecraft that lands on the surface of a planet or moon

NASA National Aeronautics and Space Administration

orbit (n) The path taken by a natural or artificial satellite in space; (v) to travel around a planet or star

orbiter A spacecraft that orbits Earth

outer planets The planets farthest from the Sun; Jupiter, Saturn, Uranus, Neptune, and Pluto

payload Cargo carried aboard spacecraft

rocket A powerful engine that propels, or boosts, a spacecraft into space

space station A large satellite aboard which people can live and work for long periods of time

surface rover A robotic vehicle that is carried to a planet or moon by a lander to collect soil samples and record images of the landscape

Index

1 2 3 4 5 6 7 8 9 0   Printed in the U.S.A. 7 6 5 4 3 2 1 0 9 8